SEA DOGGERELS

Unsung songs of the sea and more

Alan Welch

Copyright 2014 by Alan Welch
All rights reserved
ISBN 13: 978-1501058639
ISBN-10: 1501058630

Alan Welch
New Bern, North Carolina

SEA DOGGERELS
Unsung songs of sea and more

The Macon 5

On Veteran's Day 7

Mary Elizabeth Katherine Clark 8

Bay Breeze 9

Love's Charts 11

The Ballad of Composin' Bob 12

Friends 16

Dark and Stormy Night 17

Serious 19

For Kathy 20

Cajun Boy 21

We Were Great 27

Oh, Blessed Woman 28

Welcome To The New World 30

Shrimpers 31

Where the Lost Things Go 32

We The People 33

Finale Judgement 34

Good Bye 35

    I'm sometimes asked why I write (usually by the same people who ask why they bother talking to me). I wish I had an answer to this. I often think it's to amuse people and make them laugh, but then I try my hand at serious thoughts and that excuse crumbles. I guess I just like reaching people. I hope the silly stuff will make people laugh, and the serious things might give people pause for thought. I know I love the feeling when I read something to a group and they react with a laugh or a sigh.

THE MACON

I'm just a simple seaman on the schooner Major Dade,
Filled with Portland lumber bound for Oakland's building trade.
We neared the mouth of 'Frisco bay just beating down the coast,
Our sails were full, our bellies too with morning eggs and toast.

We're Captain Teague commanding and a first mate name of Twill,
A dozen able-bodies and the ship's cook at the grill.
The morning wasn't nothin' new, we'd been this way before,
Like a thousand other coastal tramps between the sea and shore.

"It's the Macon! Look, the Macon!" cried McKenzie from the bow,
And the captain bellowed angrily, "What are ye sayin' now?"
"If you've been drinkin' yet agin I'll have yer hide you swine.
I've got no berth for drunken sots on any ship of mine."

But as the captain screamed at him the rest of us looked 'round,
And each man's head was turning just as each man heard her sound.
Then off to port we see'd her just emergin' from the haze
The morning sun had lit her up as if she was ablaze.

"It's the Macon! Look, the Macon!" came the lookout's cry again,
And God she was a beauty with her silver sunlit skin.
She hung a thousand feet in California's morning skies,
And set her nose to seaward midst the startled seabird's cries.

Then cookie with a pail of slops came up from below deck,
And headed for the leeward rail then stopped to crane his neck.
He set his load down by his foot and stared into the sky,
And marveled as the shiny ship passed through the sunlit sky.

The morning dew was shimmering atop her curving flank,
It sparkled like the ripples at a lazy river's bank.
She was a gilded giant, a colossus of the air,
A stately queen a-floatin' where the others didn't dare.

"It's the Macon! Look, the Macon!" cried the lookout from the bow,
And as we stood there gaping I just had to wonder how,
A thing so big, so beautiful could share a world so poor
Where merely mortals lived below, her beauty to adore.

It's the future lads, I swear, she'll sweep us surface boats away,
And fly our cargoes through the sky by night or light of day.
And all poor sailor men like us'll have to grow us wings,
And learn to fly aboard them lovely gilded glidin' things.

She crossed our bow and headed west to join our fleet at sea,
And Teague, he swung the helm toward shore and put our stern a'lee.
And leaning 'gainst a starboard shroud I watched her out of sight,
And wondered to myself just where she might end up that night.

We tied up to the quay and let the wharf rats came on board,
And all of us worked through the night to off load every cord.
Till Duffy tuned the radio to catch the news at three,
That's when we heard them say the Macon had gone down at sea.

It was as if a round house punch had struck us to a man,
Cookie shook his head and turned back to his fryin' pan.
And me and Tucker walked back to the stern and looked to sea,
I stood there sorting through the feelings deep inside of me.

I got to see her once, it was a sight I won't forget,
But now the sight's a memory that fills me with regret
She was a thing of beauty, words can't do the job for me,
Perhaps such beauty was not meant for earthly eyes to see.

And if there's God in Heaven lads, and if he knows it's me,
There's just one favor that I ask if he's admittin' me.
I saw her once and if it isn't too much then I plea,
That Macon's still in Heaven's skies for all of us to see.

SEA DOGGERELS

On Veterans Day

The weight of centuries lays upon my bones.
Time presses down on me as heavily as does the dirt in my grave.
I never thought I would come home in a box,
Closed off from those I loved and things I wanted yet to do.
I thought this Veterans Day I would stand receiving the accolades of those whom I sought to protect.
Instead I feel the tears of those I left behind.
It's comforting that they remember.
Right they should honor the full sacrifice we made.
But how infinitely better it would be if we could celebrate it together.
I reach out and can touch others in my unit who laid their lives on the line,
And lost.
Reaching further I find others.
The gunner who died in his flaming bomber.
That sailor who drowned at sea.
A tanker who was shattered when his vehicle was blown apart.
And I feel the same dismay in them too.
I reach further and touch others, in far lands and times,
The fusilier who rode with Napoleon,
An archer who fell at Cressy,
Two sappers buried alive when their gallery collapsed in Flanders,
A Roman legionnaire cheated of retirement and citizenship,
This panzergrennadier, frozen outside of Moscow,
All wondering what their sacrifice led to.
All honored by their countries.
Each loved and remembered by their families.
All sanctified on their own particular day of remembrance.
And each of us wondering why.
And all of us thinking the best way to honor fallen veterans,
Is to ensure our children would never have to become veterans themselves.

Mary Elizabeth Katherine Clark

Oh, Mary Elizabeth Katherine Clark,
Would walk to the harbor each evening at dark.
She'd go to the harbor a sailor to seek,
To help her to pay the rent due every week.
But it's not just her plight that her clients would hark,
Smiled Mary Elizabeth Katherine Clark.

But Mary Elizabeth Katherine Clark,
Now goes to the harbor each *day* before dark.
She goes to the harbor a sailor to seek,
The reason becomes much more plain every week.
For her increasing girth is becoming quite stark,
Poor Mary Elizabeth Katherine Clark.

BAY BREEZE

When Miami's lights reflect across the waters of the bay,
And moon and neon meld as one and both would seem to say,
Forget the drugs and prostitutes, forget the poverty,
And think on how we might have been if only we could be,
The promise that the Gold Coast held fulfilled in every pass,
Instead of money laundered for the privileged upper class.
But every now and then a whiff of heaven unattained,
Will waft its way across my path and make me stop and say,
That could have been, it might have been, I wish it had'a stayed,
Instead of living only as a Buffet song he played.
And the jasmine in the bay breeze keeps on callin', callin', callin',
And the jasmine in the bay breeze calls me back to Biscayne Bay

I've dined beneath the banyan trees where hummingbirds would fly,
From orchid bloom to orchid bloom beneath an azure sky.
The perfumed breeze caressed our faces over daiquiris,
While music from the steel drum band brought back old memories.
The crushed green limestone patio was lost in paradise,
And nothing there seemed out of place to our new tourist eyes.
The lobster lunch was followed by a fine hand-rolled cigar,
While smiling faces brought our drinks from Joseph at the bar.
There's times when even jaded hearts know thanks are surely due,
To God, whose love and mercy have just showered onto you.
And the steel drum band a playin' keeps on callin', callin', callin',
And the steel drum band a playin' calls me back to St. John's town

Now Trinidad is rocky and the sea around is mud,
The Orinoco river brings the dirt to choke its flood.
But tropic birds in color sprays of plumage fantastique,
Paint the trees with rainbows which add to the isle's mystique.
With carnivale's sweet rhythms beating wildly in my soul,
And rum and Cokes in line astern begin to take their toll.
The smiles, the laughs, the swirling throngs, the costumes and the masks,
Will give a party goer every pleasure he could ask.
While Carib tastes and textures keeps one's mouth in ecstasy,
And celebration sounds drift out to where I've set to sea.
And the smell of Alma's cooking keeps on callin', callin', callin',
And the smell of Alma's cooking calls me back to Trinidad,

There's a certain sound a boat will make when gliding through the sea,
When wind and trim and current meet in perfect harmony.
And when you have each element in balance, perfect set,
As perfect as a merely human mariner can get,
The rigging starts its own sweet song, the boat itself gives voice,
And racing down before the wind your craft leaves you no choice.
She sings, I swear it happens mate, a song of joy unrolls,
As wood and steel and fiberglass take on their living souls.
And joining in the symphony you mesh with something grand,
When symbiosis lifts you up to be more than just man.
And the sea breeze in the riggin' keeps on callin', callin', callin',
And the sea breeze in the riggin' calls me back to sail again.

Love's Charts

My hours, at times o'er wind tossed sea
Like sails before a storm front flee.
When dull and sullen clouds' embrace
Obscure the moon and guide-star's face.
When home, and land's soft reveries
Seem lost and fleeting memories,
This leaves my wand'ring soul adrift
And hope is very near bereft.
When course and bearing seem to be
Just empty sockets burned in me
Your love, deep in my own heart's heart,
Is compass to the course I chart.
E're beacon, guide and gentle hope,
To guide life's ship to land's warm slope,
Back to your sweetly perfumed grace,
That gilds and garlands any place.
And makes that place a home in thee,
Which lies in loving wait for me.

The Ballad of Composin' Bob

I just paid off a steamer hauling pig iron, drills and bits,
And thought I'd spend a week or two in Frisco's fleshy pits.
I leased a flat and dropped my baggage off to get it washed,
And wandered down to Chinatown where sinful pleasures cost.

I hit a bar (or it hit me), then walked another block,
And found a seamy little dive built halfway out a dock.
It looked to be a tumbledown or shanty if you like,
The name that hung above the door was "Moose's Marlin Spike."

The air was foul with greasy smoke and smelled of beer and rot,
But the wharf rats drinking quietly seemed a friendly lot.
And as I sat and nursed a shot of rotgut rum or rye,
A seedy little tramp transfixed me with a rheumy eye.

"Here comes a touch," thinks I and sure enough he sidles up,
And begs me, "Mate, just drop a coin" into his outstretched cup.
For what you see is all that's left of talent musical,
The star crossed God's own tragedy, Composin' Bob LaSalle."

He turned away and beckoned to the barkeep dark and stout,
"I'll take my usual," he says and dumps his pennies out.
In silence we both waited 'til the drink was poured and served,
Then Bob looked up and muttered, "I had more than I deserved.

"I used to write those pretty songs that people loved to play,"
He paused and lit a cigarette; his eyes went far away.
"I lived in New York City close to Broadway's shining grands,
And wrote for stars and whiskey bars and famous big jazz bands.

"Then came my Waterloo, you see. It seemed my biggest chance —
To write a show to make a star of sweet young Laura Lance.
The girl and I, we made a pact to share the bottom line.
To seal the deal, she shared her bed and pledged her heart to mine.

"I started off just fine, you see! The Overture was grand!
The duets, trios, choruses were set to beat the band.
But when I got to Laura's big show-stopping solo piece,
I hit that writer's block stone wall: it drove me to my knees.

"She never got her break, poor thing, she always played the bits
And broke her heart in sleazy joints just singing for the tips".
He turned and looked me in the eye and withered half my soul.
"The thing is not yet run its course, and friend, you have a role."

"That song is still inside of me, I feel it hot and true,
And if you help me write it out I'll give the thing to you.
The dread song writing fever now has got me in its sway.
Paper, pen a place to think — please help me find the way."

Our fellow drinkers edged away, fear gleaming in their eyes,
But if I let this wretch go down it's me I would despise.
I turned back to the owner, then, I think his name was Moose,
"If you have a room to spare I'll pay you for it's use."

Moose nodding, said, "The door's back there," and reached beneath the bar,
And brought up pen and paper and a candle in a jar.
And like two men condemned might find their way to Hangman's Hill,
LaSalle and I walked to the back for either good or ill.

The room was small and none too clean — such things have no import,
When men must do such manly things as fight or write or sport.
A table and a chair were all the furnishings inside,
But they were all that Bob would need — well, that and writer's pride.

He sat there at the table, paper, pen and ink pot near,
Then drew a dozen breaths in deep, his mind, he said, to clear.
He grasped the pen and plunged it in the blackness of the well
And looked into the soul of him to where the musics dwell.

His hand then twitched, began to move, the nib and paper met,
And all across his brow appeared a hundred beads of sweat,
And I, God help me, mesmerized, stood witnessing too long
A sight no mortal eye should see, the writing of a song.

He made a mark and then one more, then three dots in a row,
And muttered underneath his breath of what I do not know.
Then as an avalanche accelerating down a slope,
The notes, they tumbled from his pen like sailors coiling rope.

"I got the drums!" He cried with glee, "I'll put down every note!"
And damn me for a fool, I heard the drumming as he wrote.
It was his heart, his heart I say, in syncopated beat,
Laying down the rhythm as he squirmed upon his seat.

And faster now and faster still the pen flew 'cross the page,
And notes appeared like magic as if conjured by a mage.
The notes was wrote so fast the page could hardly hold them there,
Then from the paper flew the score to whirl 'round in mid-air.

The notes they flew in circles round the table and the chair,
And started knocking into me and sticking in my hair.
They whirled 'n twirled around the room 'n pock-marked up the walls,
The noise they made was loud enough to be heard in the halls.

The whole notes, and the half notes too, did little harm you see,
The rests and pauses didn't count as they just passed right through me,
But the quarter and the eighth notes with their pointy little flags,
Were drawing blood and hurting as they tore my clothes to rags.

And Bob, God bless him, seemed to swell, to grow into his task,
"The score's complete, now for the book, Oh God, that's all I ask!"
I've sailed the seven seas and still I've never seen the like
Of writing music in the back of Moose's Marlin Spike.

Then suddenly his writing hand stopped moving 'cross the page.
The pen dropped to the table top, his face filled up with rage;
He stood and lurched against the wall, one hand aside his face,
Then horror filled his countenance and he began to pace.

"Damn me for a fool!" he cried, "and damn the English language,
And damn the music in my soul for filling me with anguish.
I'm stopped again, for in this pen and any book of knowledge,
No matter where I look at all, **THERE'S NO DAMNED RHYME FOR ORANGE!**"

He staggered back across the floor to lean above his thesis,
Then picked the score up from the top and tore it into pieces
His heart then broke, and at that stroke, I HEARD it crack, I swore.
And Bob, poor Bob, fell dead upon that dirty, unswept floor.

I'm a sailor by profession and I've seen men die before,
But as I stood there staring at that body on the floor
I couldn't help but wonder why the muse of music plays
So hard with those that love her in their own peculiar ways.

Then I heard a cough behind and turned to face the sound,
And the owner and the patrons of that bar stood all around.
"It's all right, lad," Moose gently said, "we knew it had to be.
We've waited for this day to come since nineteen thirty-three."

Moose took the paper in his hand, the rummies doffed their caps,
He held a corner to the flame and gathered up the scraps,
And when the song was ashes, as Bob's life had come to be,
We sang a hymn in honor: Rock of Ages, Cleft for Me.

Next morning found me signing on a schooner outward bound,
I hoped that where she sailed would take me far from that last sound,
But Bob's heart breaking in his chest has kept me company
And in my darkest hours showed there's those worse off than me.

He wrote his life and worldly strife was all was paid to him,
And bitter disappointment filled his cup up to the brim.
He composed away his happiness — now that he's dead I pray
He's decomposing peacefully, that's all I have to say.

Friends

To all my friends and comrades,
From here to there and back.
To all my chums and lovers,
All on my lifelong track.

To all of those who held my hand,
And those who held me back,
From making worse mistakes alone,
Than we could as a pack.

We've drunk our port and champagne,
And smoked our fine cigars.
We've eaten each other's cooking,
And carried us home from bars.

Together we counted winnings,
And tallied up our losses,
And figured out mistakes we made,
And how much they have cost us.

And if you judge a man's worth by,
The company he keeps,
Then I'm a richer man by far,
Than all the Rothschild's sweeps.

So when I get to heaven,
To Saint Peter I will say,
I'll sit right here and wait until,
My friends can find their way.

Dark and Stormy Night

T'was off the coast of Zanzibar, one dark and stormy night,
Me life was passing 'fore my eyes, my heart was filled with fright.
The sea was tossin' hard, me boys, our trusty boat was pounded,
The wind was blowin' hard enough the flying fish was grounded.

It first blew north and heeled us down and then as if to test,
She veered around and blew in even harder from the west.
And then, just when, the howling wind had reached up to a peak,
The bo'sun staggered out on deck to shout, "**We've sprung a leak!**"

"She's takin' water bad", he cried, "the pump can't keep apace,
We better drive her in to shore and find a drier place."
The captain looked at him with dread and screamed I could not hear,
But me, I knew full well just what, the captain had to fear.

For Paje port was closest on the seaward side of land,
But Paje Pearl did rule that world with sword and iron hand.
She led a band of cutthroats, evil bastards to a man,
And gave a choice of tribute, death or join her pirate band.

Now sailors is a funny lot, by dark or light of day,
And often pressed, in times of stress, you're apt to hear them say,
Of piratin' and evil men and given out their chances,
They'd choose a life a' piratin' to skip a hangman's dances.

But me, I was a cook ya see, and figured out the angles,
And thought I worked a plan to save me hide from rope end dangles.
For Pearl was said to be a girl of delicate persuasion,
Inclined to dine with proper wine on any fine occasion.

So as we made our way ashore through surf and stormy thunder,
We was beset by ruffians and quickly taken under,
They brought us to the pirate queen and lined us up in shame,
To stand in judgement for our sins before this stately dame.

The men was mostly drafted into crews aboard her craft,
Our captain, though, was spared this fate him having gone quite daft.
But I could see her snacking on some pickled figs and lime,
And knew that I could work my plan if only given time.

It finally came to my turn and her judgement fell to me,
I spoke right up quite bravely and to her I said, "Now see,
Those figs would taste much better with some cinnamon and fried,
In butter with some bacon bits and if you've never tried.

A rémoulade or quiche lorraine or chicken cacciatore",
Her eyes lit up with hunger as she listened to my story.
"My cookin' skills fill all with thrills throughout our merchant navy,
And you've not lived until you've had my deep sea squid in gravy."

Down to the kitchen I was marched and left to my devices,
There to cook a meal to please, to pleasure any vices,
And Pearl, she tasted, then she ate and then she wanted more,
I knew, then, I had won, and what my future held in store.

So now I spend my days in thrall just cookin' up a storm,
And heating up the boudoir nights to keep my lady warm.
For Pearl had fallen 'neath the spell of tasty, good nutrition,
Which placed me safe and by her side instead of in perdition.

Serious

I can't help but think it's time I stopped my being funny,
And kept away from words that play or even being punny.
And tried my hand at worthy work and have it understood,
That liberated thoughts and words could really do some good.

I want to be more relevant, yes **RELEVANT** I say,
I want my words to matter for my thoughts to finally weigh,
On one side or the other on these issues that we face,
In ever growing numbers filling up our daily space.

Other people base their works on things that really matter,
While I stand up before you spewing reams of idle chatter.
You write of war and pestilence, of agony and anguish,
While I'm content to let my thoughts just drift and doze and languish.

But can it be that sweet old me can be so mean and shallow,
That I can care so little or could be so very callow?
I turn my mind's eye inside out and scrutinize my heart,
And look into my soul's sole core, into the deepest part.

Am I a social stigma or a force for good and change,
Can I affect a modicum of enterprising range?
Eh, who is kidding who here, hmmm, I know what value be,
If I can pull a laugh from you that's good enough for me.

FOR KATHY

There are times that warm my soul
Times that make me feel all could be
 well with the world
Times that make me glad to be alive
And one of the sweetest times of all
Is when I lie beside you in bed
And wrap my arms around you
And bury my face in the scent of your hair
Your back presses soft against my chest
And your hips snuggle into the warm, welcome glove
Formed by my thighs and my stomach
And we breathe together for a precious few minutes
Then after the "Good nights"
and the caresses
and the "I love yous"
The stillness creeps in upon us
And you lie quietly in two embraces
Mine, and that of the dark
And I can feel you fall asleep in my arms
I feel the tension slip away
Like a sigh leaving your lips
The tightly wound cares
And fears
And concerns of the day
No longer play upon your thoughts
And you drift away from the world
And the worry
And from me

And it's the only time I don't resent our parting

Cajun Boy

With apologies to Justin Wilson

Now, in the bayou, way far down,
Where gator grow so fine,
An' skeeters buzz and toad frog knows
De bestest place to dine.
Dat's where our frien' the cajun boy,
He cook his stew an' all,
An' roumalade and jumbali
'N deep fry fresh fish ball.

De cajun boy, he know his spice,
to make dat food so good.

To put a tear into yo' eye an'
Have you understood.
Dat cajun food jes' don't lay dere,
An wait for you to feast,
If you don't eat it first, it think,
It might eat you at least.

Now Cajun boy he start dis dawn,
With kettle clean so good.
An' heatin' water up on top,
O' heaps an' piles o' wood.
An' when de boil be goin' fine
He add some other parts,
Some tater bits an' ol' peach pits,
An' week-old rabbit hearts.

He laff real hard an' stir it up,
An' let it come to boil,
He chuckle to hisself an' then
Sit back to let it roil.
He toss in roots an' leather boots
An' laugh 'bout cookin' soul,
Then added in a layin' hen,
An' a pre-skinned mother mole.

Dis be the bes' I ever cooked,
He thinkin' to hisself,
I better add some this n' that,
An' veggies off my shelf.
He put in greens an' magazines,
(to put some fiber in it)
An' fries onyon an' garlic cloves,
(Not long, fo' jes' a minit)

"Hoo, now de fun part here he come,"
He mutter out real sweet,
"We gots to put in spices now,
to make de meal complete."
So said, he turns an' shuffles back,
To where his spices been,
An' greets dem all by dey real name,
Like de good'n faithful frien',

Come 'ere Cayenne, hello dere dill,
How you are ol' Tobasco?
Dere's Ginger fine an' rich red wine,
An' mustard, you ol' rasco'.
Here's Basil sweet and as a treat,
Groun' pepper, black & white,
Oregano and ol' black joe,
All make dis stew jes' right.

Now 'bout dis time it smellin' fine
An' all around dere sniffin',
The muskrat, squirrel an' badger nose,
Was glad to take a whiff in.
De smell, she wafted through de wood,
An' all who smell it love it,
It wafted up to Mr. Bear.
An' circled high above it.

De smell, it go right up de nose,
O' mean ol' Mr. Bear,
"Dat do smell good", sez to 'imself,
As no one else was there.
He tarn 'is head from side to side,
An lumber off in search o',

The sweetest smell of spice an' herb,
An' meat 'n veggie combo.

In time he come up to the boy,
Whut makin all de flavor,
Who upset de natural course of things,
By cookin' up his neighbor.
De boy, he shout, "Whoa, looky here,
Don't eat me up ol' bear!"
The bear, he jes' sit back an' look.
He give him one long stare.

De bear he look an' den he sniff,
His nose don' be no fibber,
Dat stew be smellin' awful good,
De boy be all a quivver.
Den cajun boy grab up his wits,
An' tol' dat bear dis story,
How all God's critters needs to eat,
An' stew be dis boy's glory.

"You wait right der," sez Cajun Boy,
"Dis stew be nearly ready.
I gots to add a little spice,
Oh lordy, hand be steady!"
So said, de Cajun Boy pick up,
De hottest of de spices,
An' starts to add de fire below,
To his pot o' foodly vices.

Tobasco sauce, he add de jug,
Cayenne it without pause,
An' mustard, white an' yellow too,
He give it to de cause.

He vinegar an' salt de stew,
an' stir it wit a spoon,
An' hide de melted ruin,
Lest the bear see it too soon.

Now Texans claim dey chile hot,
An true enough it is,
Mexicans, dey love their spice,
But next to dis dey fizz.
De Thai food got some fire is true,
Dat whut some folk say,
But the hottest fire was ever cooked,
Was cajun's stew that day.

He scoop it up into a bowl,
An hurry to Mr. Bear.
He want to get it in de mouth,
Before th' bowl melts there.
Now Mr. Bear was greedy as
He certainly was mean,
An' with one great galumphing slurp,
He licked that ol' bowl clean.

At first he think,"Dat sure was good,
Although a little hot."
He first off thinkin' it was good,
And then he thinkin' not.
He stomach it say," Hold on here,
And "What the heck we got?"
This cain't be food, don't act like it,
It act like somethin' shot!"

About that time th' big ol' pot,
That Cajun Boy been heatin',

It melt right through an' spill de stew,
That Mr. Bear been eatin'.
The bear he watch as that ol' stew,
Et right into the ground,
An bear, he know that self same stuff,
He had jes' wolfed it down.

Now bear was mean an' greedy too,
But bear warn't no one's dummy.
He knowed that water be the cure,
For de fire down in his tummy.
So with a roar he lit right out,
'N headed fer th' lake,
An' Cajun Boy run jes as fast,
But a different trail he take.

So now you heered the story,
About Cajun's stew de jour.
An' jes how Mr. Bear found out.
How Cajun's stew could cure,
The blackest outlook Cajun Boy,
Had ever had to bear,
He lost his pot but saved his neck,
And came off on de square.

So if you ever has a feast,
Down bayou country way,
Befo' you sits down to yo' meal,
I wants to hear you say.
"Is this the stew what Cajun Boy,
Done run off Mr. Bear wiff?"
An' if it is, don' eat that stuff,
You run fast fo' de sherriff.

We got laws 'roun' dis place, I garontol you.

We Were Great

What happened to us?

We were great once.

We pulled ourselves out of the muck of the great depression.

Then we went on to forge the greatest economic powerhouse in history.

At one point we produced more than the rest of the world combined.

We rolled across Mussolini on our way to squash Hitler.

Then we kicked Tojo's ass.

We split the atom

We cured polio

We invented the internet.

We put a computer in every home.

We sent men to the moon for God's sake.

We were the shining beacon for the rest of the world to aspire to.

We were fearless.

We were mighty.

Now three people catch Ebola and the country loses its mind.

What happened to us?

Oh Blessed Woman

On a winter night in Devon,
Sure I thought I'd gone to heaven,
When I found a pub which hadn't closed it's doors.
The room was quite invitin',
With the verbal spates and fightin',
That you always find plays out 'tween wits and bores.

I was on my second pint when,
From the back, midst calls for more gin,
A Cockney bravely staggered to his feet.
He stood with arms akimbo,
Though he swayed some to and fro,
Then he straightened up and uttered this complete.

You c'n talk of your good lookers,
And your fancy gourmet cookers,
And those who paint or sculpt or sew or write.
The athelete'll tire ya,
And the business type'll fire ya,
But there's one type you can trust to treat you right.

When the winter's chill has lashed ya,
And the world outside has hashed ya,
And you only want some comfort 'neath the sheet,
When you're drifting off to dreamland,
And you cuddle up to your grand,
Blessed is the girl who's graced with nice warm feet.

Lumps of ice are not so nice, boys,
When she treats 'em like they're her toys,
And she presses them against yer back or worse.
She'll chill yer heart and knickers,
And turn your bollocks into clickers,
When she tortures you with the frozen footsy curse!

So find a woman with warm feet,
And it'll make yer life complete,
Lads, you'll wonder how you ever did without.
She'll warm yer legs, yer tush, yer back,
And make you comfy in the sack,
You'll be a happy man withall I have no doubt.

Welcome To The New World

(This is best read while snapping your fingers once a second in counterpoint time ala 1950's era hipsters. If you have a dirty sweatshirt, a black beret and cheap shades to wear even better!)

Welcome to the new world,
We got a few world leaders in the right place now Jack,
We got Ike in the White House and Tail Gunner Joe,
He's gonna fight house commies, keep us safe you know.
Know? You say? UH-huh,

We got the Ivy Leagues, we got Russian Migs,
We got filtered cigs, they're doctor approved.

Welcome to the new world,
We got a few world leaders in the right place now Jack,
We got the hippest tunes and the finest croons,
We got the best in sports, and the fairest courts,
Say? Say hey? UH-huh,

We got Disneyland, we got Stan the Man,
We got Peter Pan, they're media approved.

Welcome to the new world,
We got a few world leaders in the right place now Jack,
We got God in the class room and Jesus on our dash,
We got niggahs in their place and pockets filled with cash.
Yo? Yo-ho? UH-huh,

We got TV dinners, we got repentant sinners,
We got quiz show winners, you know the Birchers like them.

Welcome to the new world,
We got a few world leaders in the right place now Jack,
We keep buyin' in, we keep buyin' in,
We keep buyin' in, and its the same old shit!

SHRIMPERS

Give to me a strong ship,
    built to fight the sea all day,
give to me my strikers,
    unafraid to earn their pay.
Give to me my trawling nets,
    to fill with work's reward,
and I will give you shrimp enough,
    to feed a hungry horde.

I'll greet each new day's sunrise,
    with the sea breeze in my hair,
and rouse the crew to work the deck,
    in weather foul or fair.
We'll trawl the nets below,
    between the surface and the deep,
to catch the fleeting prey,
    within our net's enormous sweep.

And with our holds a-brim,
    full up, with bounty from the sea,
with aching backs and trembling arms,
    it's homeward bound we flee.
It's home to friends and family,
    to warmth and love and rest,
before we sail again, next day,
    to face another test.

Where The Lost Things Go

There's a secret, silent, hidden place, that no one knows the way,
Where all the lost and unfound things, go hide at end of day.
There's no clear path, no sign post stand, no map nor chart to show,
The wanderer, with purpose clear the proper way to go.

It's where that sock lost from its mate, the key to grandma's chest,
The lighter or that antique coin, that perfectly scored test,
Can find some quiet solitude, and rest a day or week,
But you or I can't find the way no matter how we seek.

They'll go for a vacation or a long, slow Autumn chat,
But many times decide that where they are is where it's at.
No doubt they laugh at us poor fools as we search high and low,
And never find the way they went or which way we should go.

Imagine, now, a princely realm where gobs of riches lay,
In splendor piled atop themselves and all would seem to say,
We're here, you're not and wouldn't it be fun to see once more,
Where all your treasured items go when you see them no more.

We The People

We the people, we the people, we the people,
Three little words.
Three little words that mean so much, and are heeded so little.
Three little words, what do they mean?
They mean that the vast majority of citizens want the tax code to be fair,
that everyone pays their fair share.
But the rich and huge businesses still pay little or no taxes due to loopholes.
We the people.
They mean 80% of the people in the country want better background
checks for gun purchases, and are ignored.
We the people.
They mean that more people than not want a major revamping of the
medical system so that it is affordable to get sick like in every other developed country in the world, but they are still being fought.
We the people.
They mean that over half the people in this country want unemployment to
be extended, and are not listened to.
We the people.
They mean that 90% of voters want veteran benefits to be extended.
But corporate farm subsidies are more important.
We the people.
They mean that we want corporate money OUT of the political system.
And are stymied.
We the people.
That means that few citizens want to see Social Security, that which we
have all paid into all our lives, put to risk by privatization, and still they try.
We the people.
They mean we would like to be able to choose our method of intoxication.
And pot is still (mostly) illegal.
We the people.
They mean the American dream should be open to everybody.
And it is . . . . .
Unless you are black, or gay, or a woman, or a different religion, or wear
a turban, or from a country we don't like, or speak with an accent, or are
disabled, or a veteran.
We the people. Who the hell are we?
Who indeed.

The Final Judgement

And after it was all done,
And the world of man had come to an end,
All the works of man were swept away,
Man's shadow no longer fell on the earth,
Man stood before God.
With weeping eyes he asked God why.
Why did you destroy man and all the works we've done?
Why did the mothers and the fathers,
The children, the aged,
The farmers, the workers,
The artists, the healers,
And all the multitude have to die?
Down to the last newborn infant in her nursing mother's arms?
Why are we no more?
And God answered,
I gave you more love than I gave to any other.
I made you stewards of all creation, you exploited it.
I gave you a world of beauty to enjoy, you ravaged it.
I gave you a world of diversity to fend off boredom, you enslaved it.
I gave you a world of abundance, you squandered it
      then fought over the scraps.
I gave you a brain to think with, you used it to hate each other.
I gave you imagination to create, you built ever more powerful weapons.
I gave you my son, you killed him.
I gave you my guidance, you perverted it.
It was a mistake.
Man was flawed and I could not fix him.
So it is time to try something different.
I think I'll give the Dolphins a chance.

Goodbye

I stood and watched your car roll out of sight.
You turned the corner and were gone.
Just that simple.
And quick.
You are on your drive to several states away.
Ten and a half hours of highway.
Each minute putting more miles between us.
More distance
More separation
Taking you back to West Virginia.
To friends and family.
And away from me.
And I drift off into memories of our goodbye this morning.
And slide into a reverie of thoughts about our time shared this weekend
Flush with feeling
And affections shared,
Filled with love and tenderness,
And I realize just how much I love you and am loved by you.
And though every second increases the physical space between us,
I have never felt so close to you.

SEA DOGGERELS

Additional copies can be ordered direct from:

www.alanwelch.weebly.com/writings

Thanks for stopping by, hope you enjoyed yourself.
-Alan

Printed in Germany
by Amazon Distribution
GmbH, Leipzig